CELEBRATING THE FAMILY NAME OF JACKSON

Celebrating the Family Name of Jackson

Walter the Educator

Silent King Books
a WhichHead Entertainment Imprint

Celebrating the Family Name of Jackson is a memory book that belongs to the Celebrating Family Name Book Series by Walter the Educator. Collect them all and more books at WaltertheEducator.com

USE THE EXTRA SPACE TO DOCUMENT YOUR FAMILY MEMORIES THROUGHOUT THE YEARS

JACKSON

In the folds of time, where whispers roam,

Celebrating the Family Name of

Jackson

The Jackson name stands strong, a towering dome.

A beacon of hope, in the heart's great hall,

A name that echoes, where shadows fall.

Birthed in the soil of lands so wide,

The Jacksons walked with unyielding pride.

From valleys low to mountains tall,

They faced the storm, they answered the call.

With hands that shaped the world anew,

They planted dreams, where none yet grew.

Each step they took, on paths unknown,

Was carved in stone, in hearts now grown.

Through fields of gold and rivers deep,

The Jacksons sowed what others reap.

With every dawn, their spirit soared,

In every dusk, their hearts restored.

Celebrating the Family Name of

Jackson

The name they bear, a sacred trust,

Forged in fire, immune to rust.

A bond of love, that time can't break,

A legacy pure, for future's sake.

In every branch of their family tree,

Flows a river of strength, wild and free.

Their roots run deep, in earth so kind,

With every leaf, a soul aligned.

The Jacksons know, in life's grand scheme,

That honor flows, like a gentle stream.

With every breath, they guard their own,

In every heart, a seed is sown.

From the echoes of past, they draw their grace,

With eyes set forward, they find their place.

No storm too fierce, no night too dark,

Celebrating the Family Name of

Jackson

The Jackson name, a steadfast ark.

In the quiet night, where stars align,

The Jacksons gather, in love's design.

They hold the past, in tender hands,

And build the future, on sacred lands.

The Jacksons stand, not tall but true,

In every heart, in skies so blue.

Their name a song, that time can't still,

Celebrating the Family Name of

Jackson

A melody sweet, a voice of will.

ABOUT THE CREATOR

Walter the Educator is one of the
pseudonyms for Walter Anderson.
Formally educated in Chemistry,
Business, and Education, he is an
educator, an author, a diverse
entrepreneur, and he is the son
of a disabled war veteran.
"Walter the Educator" shares his
time between educating and creating.
He holds interests and owns several
creative projects that entertain,
enlighten, enhance, and educate,
hoping to inspire and motivate you.
Follow, find new works, and stay
up to date with Walter the Educator™

at WaltertheEducator.com

Milton Keynes UK
Ingram Content Group UK Ltd.
UKHW022012230824
447344UK00012B/729